Getting It Down

Books by Judi Kesselman-Turkel and Franklynn Peterson:

The Magazine Writer's Handbook (Prentice-Hall, 1983)
Research Shortcuts (Contemporary Books, 1982)
The Grammar Crammer (Contemporary Books, 1982)
Note-Taking Made Easy (Contemporary Books, 1982)
The Vocabulary Builder (Contemporary Books, 1982)
The Author's Handbook (Prentice-Hall, 1982)
Study Smarts (Contemporary Books, 1981)
Test-Taking Strategies (Contemporary Books, 1981)
Homeowner's Book of Lists (Contemporary Books, 1981)
How to Improve Damn Near Everything around the House (Prentice-Hall, 1981)
I Can Use Tools (Elsevier/Nelson, 1981), illustrated by Tomas Gonzales
Good Writing (Franklin Watts, 1980)
Vans (Dandelion Press, 1979), illustrated by Paul Frame
Eat Anything Exercise Diet (William Morrow, 1979), with Dr. Frank Konishi
Handbook of Snowmobile Maintenance and Repair (Hawthorn, 1979)
The Do-It-Yourself Custom Van Book (Contemporary Books, 1977)

Books by Franklynn Peterson:

Children's Toys You Can Build Yourself (Prentice-Hall, 1978)
How to Fix Damn Near Anything (Prentice-Hall, 1977)
The Build-It-Yourself Furniture Catalog (Prentice Hall, 1976)
Handbook of Lawn Mower Repair (Emerson, 1973; 2nd edition, Hawthorn, 1978)

Books by Judi Kesselman-Turkel:

Stopping Out (M. Evans, 1976)

Getting It Down

How to Put Your Ideas on Paper

Judi Kesselman-Turkel
and Franklynn Peterson

Contemporary Books, Inc.
Chicago

Library of Congress Cataloging-in-Publication Data

Kesselman-Turkel, Judi.
Getting it down.

1. English language—Rhetoric. 2. Creative writing.
I. Peterson, Franklynn. II. Title.
PE1408.K557 1983 808'.042 83-10094
ISBN 0-8092-5651-7

Published by Contemporary Books, Inc.
Two Prudential Plaza, Chicago, Illinois 60601-6790
(312) 540-4500
Manufactured in the United States of America
International Standard Book Number: 0-8092-5651-7

Published simultaneously in Canada by Fitzhenry & Whiteside
195 Allstate Parkway, Markham, Ontario L3R 4T8
Canada

For our dads,

Samuel S. Rosenthal and Don C. Peterson . . .

men of ideas

Contents

TABLES AND CHECKLISTS

Getting It Down

Introduction

If you're like most students, you've had at least eight courses by now in how to write papers—and you still freeze up at some point between beginning and end in almost every paper you're assigned. You know that it's dumb to have credits subtracted for being hasty or late, yet you still deliberately postpone the inevitable until you're smack up against a due date.

It's not your fault that you freeze up; it's the system's. Almost every paper students are assigned to write is based on *ideas* and graded mostly on how well the ideas are expressed. Yet, although students are all taught how to recognize facts, they're rarely shown how to find ideas. They learn how to write paragraphs and how to structure sentences, but not where to put in the ideas. Fright is justified if you haven't been taught how to get the ideas down.

This book fills the education gap. It doesn't tell how to write paragraphs or how to structure sentences. Instead, it focuses on the main point in writing papers—filling pages with ideas. It pinpoints the basic problems, and gives step-by-step solutions.

STEP 1

Decide on Size

Before you take a dive into a strange pool, you're wise to check the depth of the water. And before you think about putting your ideas on paper, you should know how much paper to aim to fill. So the first thing to do is to decide on size.

It stands to reason that a paragraph on cars has less to say about cars than a paper on the subject, and that neither one is as complete as a book on cars. Yet few teachers stop to make the point that a brief paper on cars has to be written differently from a long paper. In order to write a paper that the grader considers outstanding (or even adequate), the first thing you must find out, or decide for yourself, is the length to shoot for.

The most specific way to describe length is in terms of word count. In some ways, it's *too* specific. It seduces you into counting words instead of focusing on ideas. But you can avoid that trap if you keep in mind that if you're assigned a 700-word paper, no grader counts every word to see if you've gone over or under by 52 words. Writing up to 10 percent over or under the suggested length is usually safe.

Because many students misunderstand what's meant by an 800-word paper and count every word before they hand it in, some teachers prefer to assign length by pages rather than word count. Figuring a paper's length by the number of pages is an extremely variable measurement. It depends on whether you type or write in longhand, on the width of your margins and the space between your lines, on whether you write big or small, even on what kind of typewriter you use. If you're given a length by pages ("Write a three-page paper"), try to get the paper-assigner to suggest how many words he'd like to see. If you can't get a word length specified, ask whether typed or handwritten pages are meant.

The standard assumption is that a typewritten page contains approximately 250 words. It does if you set your margins so that they're about 60 letters wide and then type 25 double-spaced lines to the page.

Handwriting varies a great deal. So if you turn in handwritten papers, count some pages of a previous paper to establish your usual words-to-page equivalent. If you can't memorize the number, write it down here:

I write an average of ________ words to the page.

A warning: Don't write extralarge or skip lines if you turn in handwritten papers (unless you're specifically told to do one or the other), or the grader will assume that you're padding a skimpy paper. However, there is one place that you are always permitted to skip a line, and that's between paragraphs.

1ST PROBLEM: No specific length is assigned
SOLUTION: Determine from clue words

Often, you're not told how long a paper to write. Instead you're assigned a "short theme," a "brief description," or a "term paper." Sometimes you can find out what length is expected simply by asking a direct question. Sometimes you have to make assumptions based on past assignments.

If you have absolutely no other guideline, use the following table. It's based on the actual experience of many students.

Average Expected Word Length for Papers

Paragraph: 50 to 150 words
Short paper: 150 to 350 words
Medium-sized paper: 350 to 750 words
Long paper: 800 to 1,250 words
Term paper: 1,500 to 2,500 words
Thesis: 3,000 words or more

Notice that we've purposely left out some numbers (like the numbers from 751 to 799), and overlapped others (like 150). That's to remind you that no suggested word length—even ours—should be treated as a hard-and-fast rule.

STEP 2

Tackle the Topic

You can't get ideas unless you know what to think about. In school, the "what to think about" is generally called the *topic.*

Topics don't contain verbs. They are nouns or groups of nouns, sometimes interspersed with pronouns, conjunctions, and prepositions.

A topic can be very general:

- South Carolina
- Mars
- highways
- hydrocarbons

Or it can be excruciatingly specific:

- the Apple model III computer's bookkeeping programs
- photos of Mars compared to computer-projected simulations of Mars

- the word "I" in James Joyce's *Ulysses*
- carbon tetrachloride poisoning among children

The fate of a paper is very often decided by its choice of topic. A run-of-the-mill topic earns run-of-the-mill grades, while a sexy topic makes the grader sit up and take notice. A topic that the grader likes *seems* more important, even if it's not, than one that the grader doesn't like. Biting off too big a topic can destroy a short paper by making it seem superficial or sketchy, and choosing too obvious a topic can be misconstrued as trying to avoid work. So it's important to take time choosing the right topic.

2ND PROBLEM: How to recognize an idea
SOLUTION: Compare it with fact

Before you can write about an idea, you must be able to recognize one. It's easier than you think. If a statement is not a fact, it's an idea.

A fact has been proven. An idea hasn't. Many of the things we now know are fact were once ideas:

- that the earth is round
- that the stars move
- that some mushrooms are poisonous
- that space is curved

Some ideas are so new that nobody's proven or disproven them yet:

- that porpoises may or may not be geniuses
- that vitamin C may or may not prevent colds

Some ideas that have been around a long time still haven't become fact:

- that time travel may or may not be possible

- that utopian society may or may not be achievable
- that cancer may or may not be curable

An idea becomes a fact when most of the people qualified to judge it believe it. Until then, it's only opinion. To get the judges to accept an idea as fact, the originator of the idea offers what he thinks is convincing evidence. This evidence is what's at the heart of most papers. What you're trying to prove or convince others of in your paper is the *idea.*

This is true of all factual papers. In fiction, however, you don't attempt to prove ideas but to demonstrate what you mean by them. Your demonstration is done by making the ideas come alive by cloaking them in a story.

Most ideas come to people as the result of something: of experience, of investigation, of reading or seeing or hearing. Even ideas that seem to come from nowhere (the *EUREKA!* kind) actually come from unconsciously building on something that's been seen or read or experienced. We can't give you ideas you've never had; if we did you wouldn't understand them. But we can show you where to look for ideas and how to build on what you know. That's the purpose of this book.

3RD PROBLEM: Teacher assigns too broad a topic
SOLUTION: Select an aspect of the topic

If the topic you're assigned is too general, you'll waste a great deal of research time collecting much more data than you can fit into a class paper. Then you'll spend hours deciding what to put in and what to leave out. You can't *ever* write a good paragraph on a broad topic, and even trying to write a short paper is more difficult and time-consuming if the topic is too big for it.

If a topic sounds like it could fill a book, you can assume right from the start that it's too general for any paper of less than 10,000 words. Look back at the general topics and you'll see what we mean. If you choose too specific a topic, you won't have enough to write about, but for now it's better to err on the side of being specific. When you get to outlining your paper, you can broaden the topic quite easily if you discover that you can't fill the size paper you're supposed to write with the topic you've selected.

A teacher's list of assigned topics is often very general. It's easier to sound brilliant if you offer lots of catchy details and several convincing conclusions on a narrow subject, than if you take broad and superficial strokes at a subject that's too general. The trick is to find an interesting *aspect* of the assigned topic to write about.

You can often create an aspect of a general topic merely by adding another noun to it.

Assignment: Write about South Carolina
Some acceptable topics:

- South Carolina trees
- South Carolina's government
- volcanoes in South Carolina
- books about South Carolina
- inventors from South Carolina

Assignment: Write about highways
Some acceptable topics:

- highway improvement
- highway pavement
- highway paints
- highway signs
- highway accidents
- highway police
- highway robbery

Adding an adjective to a specific aspect of a general topic makes it an even more specific assignment:

- South Carolina's evergreen trees

- South Carolina's blighted trees
- South Carolina's historic trees
- future highway improvement
- past highway improvement
- unneeded highway improvement

When a topic already sounds quite specific, it may seem to a teacher as if you're hair-splitting if you get more specific by adding more nouns. In that case, try adding adjectives or modifying phrases:

Assignment: Write about programs for the Apple computer
Some acceptable topics:
- future programs for the Apple computer
- word processing programs for the Apple computer
- programs specifically designed for the Apple computer

Assignment: Write about the word "I" in James Joyce's *Ulysses*
Some acceptable topics:
- the word "I" in the first chapter of *Ulysses*
- the word "I" as used by Molly Bloom in *Ulysses*

Sometimes you're assigned a broad topic but are told to deal with an aspect of it. In that case, you're *expected* to break the topic into smaller topics and write about one of them. But if the topic you're given is already quite specific, don't look for trouble by trying to make it more specific. You can add your own touch of brilliance when it comes to choosing your approach to that topic.

4TH PROBLEM: The assigned topic is boring
SOLUTION: Find an interesting aspect

If you're given a boring topic, you can often make it more interesting by choosing a specific aspect that interests you.

For example, if you're a hockey player and have to write a paper about inflation, you might use the salaries of hockey players to make your points about inflation:

Assigned topic: inflation
Your topic: Inflation and Hockey Players' Salaries

Clever students take their cues from the course instructor and choose something she too is interested in or would like to know more about. Unless your teacher is particularly sensitive to apple-polishing, this is the way to go for top grades. Here's where you can look for clues to shared interests:

First check your class notes. Does one small side issue keep showing up? For example, are there several references in your economics notes to clever illegal schemes? Make the topic of your paper on inflation "Clever Illegal Schemes in Inflationary Times."

Are there lots of notes in your modern poetry notebook that refer to classical mythology? The teacher said these things because he was interested in them and you may have taken the notes on these side issues because they interested you, too. Work classical mythology into your topic.

Listen to the lectures. The same rule of thumb can be applied. Does the physics prof get into biographical asides about the great discoverers? It's a sure bet she likes to read biographical sketches.

Physics assignment: Write about quantum energy
Your topic: The Discoverer of the Quantum Particle

Does the French teacher talk a lot about French culture? That's probably his bag. Can you make it yours?

French assignment: Write about the French Alps
Your topic: Folk Songs in the French Alps

If you're given a boring list of specific topics to choose from, and the assignment calls for anything but a short paper or a paragraph, don't fall into the trap of selecting one topic because it looks like it requires the least amount of research. If you think that topic looks a lot easier to write about than the rest, it's for one of two reasons: (1) you already know a lot about it, which means it probably does interest you the most and you can write about it well with a minimum of research, or (2) you're underestimating the quality of the paper the teacher wants on that topic and you'll probably bomb because of underresearching.

5TH PROBLEM: You don't know anything about the topic
SOLUTION: Do some preliminary research

If you know zilch on the assigned topic, don't try to even think about it before you do some reading. For a short- or medium-sized paper, a half hour with a good encyclopedia is enough. For a long paper, a term paper, or a thesis, you should put in three hours of skimming through journals or books.

Don't take notes when you're doing this research. Keep in mind that you're just looking for a general understanding of the topic. But do make note of particularly good references to come back to.

Some good quick sources for preliminary research are:

- encyclopedias
- abstracts in the subject area (for example, *Psychology Abstracts*)
- references found in *Reader's Guide to Periodical Literature*
- *Facts on File*
- *The New York Times Index*

For other suggestions, see a good book on research skills, such as our companion volume *Research Shortcuts.*

6TH PROBLEM: You've got to find your own topic
SOLUTION: Take an inventory of your interests

If you can choose *any* topic for a particular assignment, select something you'd either like to tell others about or know a good deal about yourself. Here are some broad topics to get you thinking about specifics.

- a hobby
- a personal experience
- a person or group of people you're familiar with
- an illness
- a place
- a decision
- a theory

Most open-ended assignments are given in creative writing classes. In those classes, the emotional impact of your writing often counts for more with the grader than the quantity or quality of your ideas. To get emotion into your writing, choose a specific topic that you feel strongly about, whether it's a scary fire that you saw or a candidate for political office that you don't support.

If you're writing fiction, the rule for creative papers applies: choose a topic you can get emotional about. Some broad fiction topics are romance, science fiction, animals, and adventure. An example of a specific topic for an adventure story is a death-defying adventure on a mountain face.

Take several minutes right now to choose a tentative topic. If there's no paper hanging over your head at the moment, select a topic for some class anyway so that you can get some real practice as you follow along in this book.

STEP 3

Adopt an Approach

We said before that the point of writing papers is to express *ideas,* but until now we've been talking about *topics,* not ideas. You can't have any ideas until you know what to have them about. But in order to write a paper, you've got to know how you're going to approach the topic. The topic combined with the way you approach it is your paper's *main idea.* Choose a clever or interesting main idea, and develop it cleverly and interestingly, and you'll get an A. But try to write before you've got your approach figured out, and you'll have trouble even getting started.

You can show your approach to a topic (often called the *angle* by published writers) by adding verbs that tell *what's going on* with the topic, and also by linking your topic with certain specific key words like *how to, personal experience,* and *history.*

Topic: a death-defying adventure on a mountain face

Approach: personal experience
Combined: My Death-Defying Adventure on a Mountain Face

Topic: South Carolina evergreen trees
Approach: how to
Combined: How to Recognize South Carolina Evergreen Trees

Topic: interstate highway improvement
Approach: history
Combined: The History of Interstate Highway Improvement Programs

Notice that the main idea of the paper also makes a good title for it. This is so generally true, you can test whether you've got a good main idea by asking yourself if you've come up with an attention-getting title. We'll give you some guidance with that in Step 4.

7TH PROBLEM: You can choose any approach and you don't know where to start
SOLUTION: Select from the five basic approaches

Choosing an approach is even harder than choosing a topic if you don't know where to begin. There seems to be an infinite number of ways of looking at anything. In reality, however, all the ways can be classified into five major categories:

1. giving directions
2. reporting events
3. explaining ideas
4. persuading
5. inventing a story

The first four categories are all nonfiction approaches; the fifth is fiction.

It's perfectly acceptable (and often impressive) to deal with more than one category in a paper—for example, to describe something in a persuasive paper, or to report an event that illustrates an idea you're explaining. Later on we'll let you know when to stick in any secondary angles you'd like to include. But now's the time to choose just one main approach. It will practically guarantee that your paper makes a point and sticks to it, and that's important.

To help you choose the best angle, let's review all five of them.

1. YOU'RE GIVING DIRECTIONS

Papers that give directions are all around us, from the instructions on paint cans to the how-to articles in popular magazines. *How to* is often part of the title. In school, *how-I-did-it*s and *how-they-did-it*s are more often written than *how-to-do-it*s. If you've ever based a science research paper on one of your own experiments, you've done a *how-I-did-it.* Even the lowly science lab report belongs in this category.

In addition to the papers that offer directions on how to do something *tangible,* this category includes papers that describe *intangible* courses of action: how to cope with stress, how to understand electronic music, how to "keep your head when all about you are losing theirs and blaming it on you. . . ."

It's a good idea to choose an out-and-out *how-to* angle for your topic only if you've had personal experience with it. It's dangerous to give instructions to other people if you haven't done the thing yourself. One of our students once turned in a paper on using truss frames in building houses, when she'd never even erected a dollhouse or fixed a stuck door. Her research got all the facts right, but her writing jumbled them in an order that made no sense. In addition, because she couldn't herself picture what she was describing, she couldn't describe very accurately how the trusses went together in a way that made sense to other people.

The *how-it-works* paper is also a member of this category. Instead of a how-*to-do*-it, this is a how-*it-does*-it: a paper that describes a standard, recurring set of events. Examples are papers that show how an engine drives a car or that describe the life cycle of a frog.

The quickest way to approach your topic from a direction-giving angle is to add the words *how to.* Starting with the seven general topics listed on page 13, we show you, in the chart on page 18, how easy it can be.

2. YOU'RE REPORTING EVENTS

The report tells, as impartially as possible, about one or more things that have happened. It covers at least several of the following aspects: *what* happened, *how* it happened, *when* it happened, *where* it happened, *who* it happened to, and *why* it happened. In other words, it's a *history.* But it may come disguised as very recent history, such as a news article, a police report, a social worker's report, an insurance adjuster's report, or a sales report by the branch office manager to his boss.

If you decide that you want to approach your topic as a report, you can do it easily. Just put *Report, Research Report,* or *History* in the title—or tack on some *past-tense* verbs that show that you're going to describe things that have already happened.

If you're reporting on events that you yourself have lived through, it's a good idea to write your paper as a *personal experience* or *reminiscence* instead of a history, since the paper-marker will expect the reporting to be biased anyway. To show that it's personal experience, add the clue word *I.*

Starting again with the seven general subject areas listed on page 13, notice, in the chart on page 19, how easy it is to make them into reports. Note especially the words that show that we're dealing with a *continuing past series of events*—they are in heavy type.

General Topic	*More Specific Topic*	*Aspect Added*	*With Angle Added*
a hobby	skiing	cross country	How to Ski Cross-Country
an experience	my vacation	working	How I Spent My Vacation Working at Yellowstone
people	movie stars	hometown	How to Become a Hometown Movie Star
illness	the flu	symptoms	How to Recognize the Flu
a place	sea bottom	fish	How Fish Survive at the Bottom of the Sea*
a decision	voting	for candidates	How to Decide between Candidates
a theory	capitalism	if you're poor	How to Become a Capitalist without Owning a Dime

* This is a how-it works.

General Topic	*More Specific Topic*	*Aspect Added*	*With Angle Added*
a hobby	skiing	place, time, conditions	Ski Conditions in Vermont, **1978–83**
an experience	my vacation	worst fright	The Worst Fright I **Had** on My Vacation
people	movie stars	place, decline	The **Decline** of the American Movie Star
illness	the flu	a new vaccine	**Research Report** on a New Flu Vaccine
a place	sea bottom	shipwreck	How the Titanic **Sank** to the Sea Bottom
a decision	voting	the South, voters' rights	A **History** of the Southern Voters' Rights Movement
a theory	capitalism	place	How Capitalism **Rose** in Japan

3. YOU'RE EXPLAINING IDEAS

The first two approaches that we discussed involved things that could be *seen:* places, people, objects, events, actions. Although all the papers that fall into those two categories have main ideas, their content rarely has anything to do with what people generally consider to be ideas. The paper that *explains* deals largely with at least several abstract ideas—and it's the kind that instructors are most fond of assigning. The more abstract or complicated the main idea you choose to explain, the greater the number of subordinate ideas you'll have to include and the longer a paper you'll need in order to do it. So if you're assigned to write a short paper, or have decided on a short one, select a simple idea.

Here's a simple idea:

Rich People Aren't Always Honest

Here's a complicated one:

Dishonesty Can Result from Environmental or Genetic Causes

The first idea can be explained adequately with as few as three simple examples of dishonest rich people (although you could write 10,000 words on the idea if you needed to). For the second idea, you must tell what you mean by the abstract words *environmental* and *genetic* before you can even begin to discuss your main idea.

A good guide to complexity is to ask yourself how many abstract words you have in your topic. The fewer the abstractions, the simpler your paper will be to write.

Some effective ways to make a topic into an explanatory paper are to describe it, to show cause and effect, to give pros and cons, and to describe assets and liabilities—or you can ask a question about the topic. It's easy to write an explanatory paper if the topic is an abstract idea; it's much harder to write about a tangible thing. Usually, the latter ends up being a description, which is really a *how-it-works.*

Taking the seven general subject areas listed on page 13, let's make explanatory papers of them. (See the chart on page 22.) Try your hand at making other explanatory papers from the same topics.

4. YOU'RE PERSUADING

Persuasion (sometimes called *argument*) is like explanation in that you're writing about ideas. But there's an added element: your own point of view. Unless you're assigned a persuasive paper, we suggest that you tackle it only if you like to take on challenges. If you take a common, established point of view (for instance, the view that voting preserves good government), the grader's first reaction will be, "So what else is new?" and you'll have trouble getting even a B. On the other hand, if you take a controversial point of view (for instance, that voting does nothing to ensure good government), you'll have a shot at an A, but you're going to have to offer some really powerful evidence in order to earn that grade. And you've not only got to convince, but you've got to remember to discuss—and refute—the opposition point of view as well.

Most persuasive papers, as well as explanatory papers, depend on *fact,* not *opinion,* to convince the readers. Unless opinion (also called *value judgment*) is specifically asked for in the assignment, keep it out of your actual paper. But it should show up in the point of view you take when you're presenting facts, because in the course of deciding what to put in and what to leave out, you must bring your own value judgment to your topic and approach. *Good, bad, poor, wealthy, coddled,* and such are value judgments.

Consider a paper called "How Lincoln Used Good Public Relations, but Poor Military Strategy, in the Civil War." If it were full of your own opinion of how well Lincoln did as a

General Topic	*More Specific Topic*	*Aspect Added*	*With Angle Added*
a hobby	skiing	effects	How Skiing Affects the Heart
an experience	my vacation	*	*
people	movie stars	pros and cons	Are Movie Stars Good Actors?
illness	the flu	cause	Why Children Get the Flu So Easily
a place	sea bottom	explanation	Why the Sea Bottom Is Mountainous
a decision	voting	assets and liabilities	Does Voting Result in Good Government?
a theory	capitalism	explanation	How a Capitalist Society Functions

*Notice that an explanatory paper can't be written about a personal experience. Notice also that we can write explanatory papers about movie stars by turning them into an abstract concept instead of living people, and can do the same with skiing by turning it, too, into a concept (sport). However, our explanatory papers about the flu and the sea bottom are really compilations of research reports with an explanatory angle as the main focus (see page 27).

politician and military strategist, the grader would (or should) scrawl across it, "You're no expert. Where's your proof?" But if it consisted largely of facts and experts' opinions that bolstered your point of view, you'd have a strong argument for your hidden opinions.

Reviews are persuasive papers that *do* include your opinions along with the facts that support them. Book critiques and movie reviews are in this category. When you're writing reviews, you must never try to disguise your opinions as fact.

Taking some explanatory papers used for previous examples, let's turn them into persuasive papers. Try your hand at other kinds of persuasion using the same topics.

Explanatory Paper	*Persuasive Paper*
How Skiing Affects the Heart	Skiing Is Good for the Heart
Are Movie Stars Good Actors?	Few Movie Stars Are Good Actors
Why Children Get the Flu So Easily	Children Wouldn't Get the Flu So Easily if They Weren't Mollycoddled
Does Voting Result in Good Government?	Voters Don't Know How to Choose Good Representatives
How a Capitalist Society Functions	Capitalist Societies Make the Rich Richer

5. YOU'RE INVENTING A STORY

A short story depends on facts as much as a factual paper does. You can't make your characters, setting, or story convincing unless they seem real. Even the outer-world creatures of space movies behave like real humans or animals. By the same token, you must choose an approach to the topic of your short story before you can begin it.

The approach, here, is the point you want to make about

the topic you've chosen. It doesn't always appear in the title, but you need to know it before you can write the story, since it's shown in the climax—and everything, from the story's first sentence, leads to its climax.

Here are some examples of short story approaches.

Story	*Topic*	*Approach*
The Gift of the Magi (O. Henry)	giving gifts	the most important gift is love
The Cask of Amontillado (Poe)	revenge and horror	revenge is sweetest when the victim leads himself into the trap
The Snows of Kilimanjaro (Hemingway)	a man dying on a mountain top	death can be a rescue

8TH PROBLEM: Confusion over what *abstract* means
SOLUTION: Check the word against your senses

Nouns, verbs, and adjectives can all be concrete or abstract, but since ideas consist mostly of noun words, we'll stick to nouns here. The simplest explanation for the difference between concrete and abstract nouns is the one you may have learned in school:

1. Proper nouns (*Chattanooga, John Brown,* the *President*) are always concrete.
2. Common nouns can be either concrete or abstract. Concrete nouns name physical, visible, tangible objects such as *dog, town, water;* abstract nouns name ideas that can't be seen, touched, smelled, tasted, or heard.

All this is true. But there are many words that aren't easy to separate into abstract and concrete. *Lullaby* is considered concrete, but *music* is listed in some grammar books as abstract. A *vote* is considered concrete, but a *referendum* is considered abstract. Actually, for many ideas there's a continuum of words that express it, going from the very abstract to the very concrete—and the most concrete words are most often used in their adjective forms. The in-between words are somewhat concrete and somewhat abstract. For many ideas, we can draw diagrams that look a lot like family trees, showing levels of concreteness or abstractness. Here's one for the idea *resolve* (a very abstract idea) that shows a number of its synonyms in increasing order of concreteness:

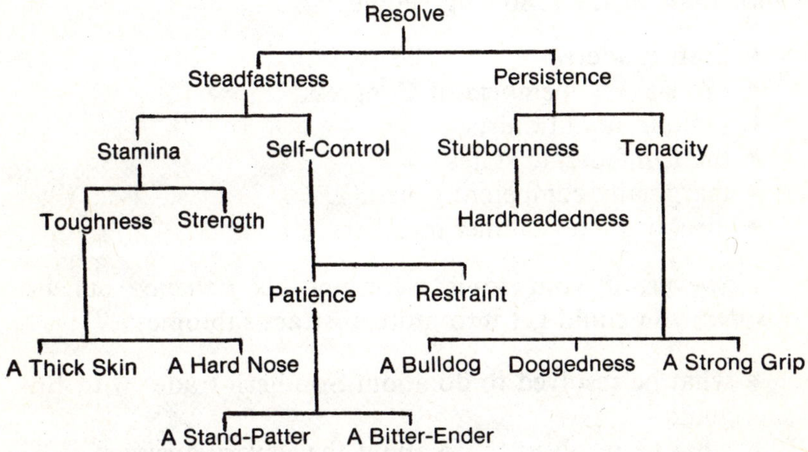

Resolve is the most abstract word. *Steadfastness* and *persistence* are a bit less abstract: the first means "active resolve" and the second means "passive resolve." The third level adds more concreteness to the *resolve* idea: *stamina* and *self-control* suggest subtle distinctions between bodily resolve and spiritual resolve, while *stubbornness* and *tenacity* show slightly different shades of *persistence*. By the time we reach the bottom line, the once-abstract, once-general idea is so precisely defined that it narrows down to the most specific meaning possible for each kind of *resolve.* Almost every word is concrete enough to make you see, hear, feel, taste, or smell it: *thick skin, hard nose, bitter-end, stand-patter, hard-headedness, a bulldog, doggedness, a strong grip.*

The point of this diagram is to show why writing a paper about *patience* requires less explanation of what you mean than writing a paper about *resolve.* It's a less abstract idea because it has a more narrowly defined meaning.

If, for example, you were to write an adequate paper based on the topic "Abe Lincoln's Patience during the Civil War" you'd probably have to cover his very specific patience with some of the following people:

- draft evaders
- pro-slavery members of Congress
- militant abolitionists
- the Confederate states
- marginally competent generals
- insubordinate cabinet members

However, if your topic were not his *patience* but his *resolve,* you could get into more abstract subtopics:

- what he resolved to do about Southern trade with England
- what he resolved to do about the slavery question
- how he resolved to change military tactics
- how he resolved to overlook public opinion
- how he resolved to handle international diplomacy

If you need a more concrete or abstract word that narrows or expands *your* idea, look up your tentative word in any good thesaurus. That's where all the synonyms in our word tree come from. Having a thesaurus handy not only helps you dig deeper into your topic; it also gets your idea juices flowing.

9TH PROBLEM: You want to tackle two approaches
SOLUTION: You'll need to write a longer paper

The explanatory paper on *why the sea bottom is mountainous* contains two angles. Before you can explain *why,* you have to show that it *is* mountainous. The *why* is still unverified theory. However, the fact that it *is* mountainous can be shown by proven past research in a *report.* To include both the report and the explanation, you must write a longer paper than if you were just taking one angle. Usually it can't be done well in less than 800 words.

You'll almost always need to include two approaches if your *why* or *how* paper deals with an idea that's not common knowledge. For instance, the persuasive paper *voters don't know how to choose good representatives* hides a secondary angle: *how voters choose representatives.* You're going to have to write a how-it-works before you get to your persuasive arguments.

If you have to use two approaches in one paper, you must decide before you begin which angle is part of your *main idea* and which one is secondary. The main idea is the one you want the reader to remember when she's finished reading your entire paper.

A long paper may deal with two aspects of one topic, for instance *buying watches in China* and *buying watches in America.* That's not the same as having two approaches, as in the example *why the sea bottom is mountainous.* Papers with multiple topics should approach them all from the same angle. The specific approach is usually a *comparison:* buying watches in China compared to buying watches in the United States.

We'll soon talk about outlining, and then you'll see how secondary angles are worked into a paper. For now, if you've written them into your approach, take them out unless you intend to write a long paper.

10TH PROBLEM: You're assigned a specific approach but you're not sure what it means
SOLUTION: Categorize the approach

There are many words that describe how you can deal with a topic, and sometimes an assignment includes one of those telltale words:

- Tell your *impressions* of Oliver Twist.
- *Compare and contrast* the civil war and the revolution.
- *Defend* the statement, "Might makes right."

Often these descriptions are verbs (*compare and contrast, tell, defend*), but sometimes you're more likely to spot a telltale noun first (for instance, *impressions,* which is shorthand for "how it impresses you"). The one thing they have in common is that they all show *what approach you're to take to the topic.*

,These words of approach can be very confusing at first because they make it seem as if there are a thousand ways of dealing with a topic. Actually, they all fit into one of the five categories named earlier: giving directions, reporting events, explaining ideas, persuading, or inventing a story. Although not all teachers agree on exactly what the words mean, the following chart will help you decide what's being asked for. (If the approach you're assigned isn't included here, look for its synonym or antonym.)

Words Commonly Used to Show Approach

Word or Phrase	*Approach Suggested*
assets and liabilities	explanation
compare	explanation
contrast	explanation
criticize	explanation (if about an idea) opinion paper (if about a thing)

Words Commonly Used to Show Approach (continued)

Word or Phrase	*Approach Suggested*
critique	opinion paper
defend	persuasion
define	explanation
describe	explanation (if about an idea) direction paper (if about a thing) report (if about a past event)
discuss	explanation
disprove	persuasion
distinguish	explanation
does ________?	explanation
evaluate	opinion paper
explain	explanation
give your opinion of ______	opinion paper
how does ________?	explanation
illustrate	explanation
impressions	personal experience (report) or personal opinion
justify	persuasion
outline	explanation (if about an idea) report (if about an event)
personal experience	report
pros and cons	explanation
prove	persuasion
reminiscence	report
report	report (if about past events) explanation (if about ideas)
research and report on	how-I-did-it (if a lab report) how-they-did-it (if about things) report (if about events) explanation (if about ideas)

Words Commonly Used to Show Approach (continued)

Word or Phrase	*Approach Suggested*
review	report (if about events) explanation (if about ideas) also used for opinion papers
show how, show the cause, show the effect	explanation (if about ideas) report (if about events)
show how to	direction-giver
show how ________ works	explanation (if about an idea) direction-giver (if about a thing)
summarize	explanation (if about an idea) report (if about a thing)
tell, tell why, tell how	usually explanation
tell how ________ happened	report
trace	usually a report
why does ________?	explanation

STEP 4

Test the Title

The three things worth the most points in any paper's grade are (1) having a clear theme (another word for *main idea*), (2) sticking to it, and (3) saying enough about it. For keeping your theme manageable and firmly at the forefront of your mind, nothing works as well as a good working title.

If you've taken enough time to narrow your topic and add your approach, you already have a good working title and can take some time now to stand up and stretch or get something to eat. You've probably noticed that every phrase in the last column of our previous charts becomes a title just by capitalizing the appropriate letters.

Before you stretch, though, take a look at the title you created.

1. *Does it allow you to include everything you want to deal with in the size paper you're attempting?* If it covers some elements that you don't want to cover, narrow the topic some more. If it doesn't cover some of

the things you want to talk about, broaden it a little. You'll have another chance to check it against size when you get to outlining.

2. *Does it incorporate the one main angle you've decided on—explaining, persuading, reporting, giving directions, or inventing a story?*

If you can answer yes to both questions, you've earned a short break.

11TH PROBLEM: You're not sure whether the title covers certain ideas
SOLUTION: For borderline ideas, think about size and approach

Everyone knows not to include skiing in a paper about the post office, or cost accounting in a paper about the sunset. But until you have a working title and know the paper's size, it's hard to decide which borderline ideas belong. For instance, try answering these questions before you read on:

- *Should you discuss tar content in a short paper on cigarette smoking?*
- *Should you discuss running in a long paper on jogging shoes?*
- *Do current postal rates belong in a thesis on the post office?*
- *Does the price of gold fit into a paper on double-digit inflation?*

It's impossible to know whether your answer is right or wrong until you've got a working title. Just look at how easy it suddenly becomes when you ask the same questions once you know length and theme.

Should you discuss tar content in a short paper called

"Cigarette Smoking is Dangerous to Your Health?"

It's pretty clear now that tar content should be discussed even if the paper's very short, since tar content is an important part of the danger.

Should you discuss tar content in a short paper called "A History of the Times Square Cigarette-Smoking Sign?"

It's easy to see that there's no reason to get into tar content at all even if the paper is 10,000 words long.

Should you discuss running in a long paper called "Why Jogging Shoes Were Invented?"

No matter what the paper's length, you'll have to discuss the reason for the invention: to help people run better.

Should you discuss running in a paper called "Are Running Shoes Good for the Feet?"

You need not discuss running at all (though you may get into it in a long paper). Instead of the shoes' effect on *running,* you'll concentrate on their effect on the *runner.* Notice how this title keeps you from talking about the runner's state of mind, too. You're focused just on the runner's feet.

Do current postal rates belong in a thesis called "How the Federal Government Divested Itself of the Post Office?"

Postal rates don't belong even if you're writing a book on this idea. But they do belong in a paper called "How the Post Office Fights Inflation," unless you've got better examples to use.

Does the price of gold fit into a short paper called "Causes of Double-Digit Inflation?"

If you have evidence that the changing price of gold affects inflation, gold is a good example to use in your paper. But if you've found that it's the other way around (that inflation affects the price of gold), forget it, since your paper—no matter what its size—doesn't deal with inflation's impact on other parts of the economy. (In order to work that information into your paper, you could change the working title to "How Double-Digit Inflation Affects the Price of Gold.")

As you can see, besides keeping you on track, a good working title helps cut down on your research time, because you won't be hunting down lots of information that doesn't belong within the parameters of your paper.

STEP 5

Pick a Point of View

We've shown that the *persuasive* paper has an obvious point of view. Its very format is an argument for one side or the other in an issue in which neither side has yet been proven wrong. But actually, it's impossible to write *any* paper without a point of view—whether you know you have it or not. And everyone's point of view is different, because no two writers think the same way about any idea. Even if you and a friend start with the same main idea and the same research materials, the facts you select to include will be different from the ones your friend chooses. (If they aren't, one or both of you is surely going to get an F for plagiarism.)

If you deliberately form a strong attitude toward the main idea after you research* but before you write your paper, the parts of the paper will actually be much easier to select and arrange. In addition, a paper with a clear, consistent point of view has the punch, the vitality, and the sense of uniqueness that earn A's.

---

*To explain how to research quickly and well would take up a book by itself. If you need help, get the companion volume *Research Shortcuts.*

12TH PROBLEM: Confusion between approach and point of view
SOLUTION: Separate logic from emotion

Look back at the five basic approaches listed on page 15. All of these words are "show and tell" words. They all give concrete, objective, logical directions for what you're to do with an idea. On the other hand, words that show *point of view* are opinion words. They're based on emotion, not logic. They make subjective value judgments. *Good, bad, poor, wealthy, coddled, generous, difficult, better,* and *worse* are some examples. Look back at the section on persuasive papers to see how they're included in some titles.

But take the innocuous title for the direction-giving paper, "How to Study More Effectively." To write a convincing paper, its author must take a point of view: that some people don't study effectively enough, that they can learn, and that she can teach them within the confines of the paper. Unless she makes those assumptions, she won't know where to start and the result will sound disorganized, pointless, and wishy-washy.

In the above example, the writer's choice of title gave her a clue as to what point of view would be best for her paper. Some titles give no clues at all. Here's an example: "Ski Conditions in Vermont, 1978–83." It sounds like it ought to be just a straightforward collection of five-year data. But if you were writing it:

- Which months' data would you include? What if you discovered that the ski season started earlier or ended later one year?
- Did you collect data from resort ski hills or from local park ski hills? If you got both kinds, you're going to have to decide if they can be lumped together or if the local parks' hills are less or more important, taking into consideration the fact that most resorts make their own

snow if natural conditions are poor.

- How are you defining "conditions"? Did your research turn up just snow conditions or did you get weather conditions too? Did you find some other conditions that you'd like to mention in the paper?

There are no right and wrong answers to these questions. What you include and what you leave out depend on your interpretation of the assignment you've given yourself; in other words, on your point of view.

13TH PROBLEM: Confusion between aspect and point of view
SOLUTION: Aspect is factual, while point of view is opinion

Aspects of a topic are often written as adjectives:

evergreen trees of South Carolina

Points of view are also often expressed as adjectives:

pampered children get the flu

But you'll never confuse one with the other if you remember the difference between *fact* and *opinion.* That some trees are evergreen is proven fact. That some children are pampered is opinion. Aspect is fact. Point of view is opinion. It's as simple as that.

Before looking at the answers, test yourself on whether the italicized words below show aspect or point of view:

1. The *Worst* Fright of My Vacation
2. *Future* Programs for the Apple Computer
3. The *Easy* Road to Success
4. The *Complete* Guide to Home Repair
5. How to *Take Care* of Your Dog
6. The *Decline* of the American Movie Star

Here are the answers:

1. *Worst* is opinion: point of view
2. *Future* is fact. The future has been proven to exist.
3. *Easy* is opinion: point of view
4. *Complete* is also opinion, since completeness is a personal assessment.
5. *Take Care* isn't point of view or aspect. It's the writer's approach. (The fact that it's a verb should have given you a clue.)
6. *Decline* is also approach. It's just the kind of past-history word that's sometimes used in reports. (You would have had no doubts about this if the title had been "The Decline in Gross National Product between 1982 and 1983.")

14TH PROBLEM: Graders look for originality
SOLUTION: Combine unusual ideas, topics, and approaches

If you're writing a report or are giving directions, nobody expects much originality—just a clear picture of what happened or what to do. But if you're writing an explanation, a persuasion, or a short story, originality is what earns A's. So check to see whether what you've got is original or just a rehash of what you've read or heard.

Most students think that an *original* thought has to be *unique*. That's not true at all. Few thoughts have never been thought before. An idea that was first thought up centuries ago can be original—so long as you got the idea independently, without having read or heard about it. While James Watson was puzzling out his Nobel prize-winning DNA replica in Cambridge, England, Linus Pauling was independently solving the same puzzle in California, just a few steps behind. Watson won the prize because he got his paper in print first. But Pauling's achievement wasn't any less outstanding.

The idea of what DNA looks like didn't come to either Watson or Pauling out of the blue. These scientists conceived it by combining what they already knew. Most original ideas come about in one of three ways:

1. by combining two or more old ideas that were not combined before (at least not to your knowledge)
2. by approaching an old topic in a new way
3. by tackling an old topic and approach from a fresh point of view

It's easy to combine two old ideas to get an original one. To show how, we'll take two ideas at random that have already been suggested:

How Capitalism Rose in Japan

How Skiing Affects the Heart

Combining these, we might come up with:

Did Skiing's Effect on the Heart Influence the Rise of Capitalism in Japan?

As you can see, many original ideas are outlandish. But take two ideas in the same subject area, and you often come up with an excitingly original thesis. These two ideas were read in books:

T. S. Eliot's poetry is a lot like Ezra Pound's

Eliot and Pound were friends

Together, they formed this new thesis:

T. S. Eliot's Friendship with Ezra Pound Influenced His Poetry [or the other way around]

The second way to get originality is to take a new approach to an old topic. Let's take a random topic and add some words that show approach.

TOPIC: The Southern Voters' Rights Movement

1. *Approach word:* worst
   Idea: The Worst Thing about the Southern Voters' Rights Movement
2. *Approach word:* how to
   Idea: How to Form a Southern Voters' Rights Movement Today
3. *Approach word:* why
   Idea: Why a Southern Voters' Rights Movement Was Needed

The third path to originality is to take a novel point of view. For instance, let's assume that everyone is given the same topic to write about:

How Communal Societies Work

If your point of view is that they don't always work, you might turn in one of the following papers:

1. How Communal Societies Work in Fiction but Not in Fact
2. How Communal Societies Work for Primitive People but Not for Civilized People
3. How Communal Societies Work in Austere Times but Not during Prosperity

If the assigned topic is "A New Cure for Cancer," and you maintain the point of view that cancer isn't generally curable, you needn't change the title at all. But an important subtopic in your paper could be:

Past "Cures" that Were Later Shown Not to Work

In addition, you could demonstrate—with your evidence—that not all experts agree that this particular "cure" is in fact a cure.

If the assigned title is "How to Patch Plaster Walls" and you hold the point of view that it's a messy job, some of the subtopics in your paper could be:

1. What to Do When the Patching Plaster Sticks Your Fingers Together
2. How to Clean Up the Spill on the Floor
3. How to Get the Stuff Out of Your Hair When You're Done
4. How to Find a Pro Who'll Come in to Repatch Your Unsightly Patch-Up Job

This example shows that it's point of view, more often than topic or approach, that can successfully turn an otherwise serious paper into a howler.

In addition to being *original,* your idea must be *defensible.* You must be able to convince the grader that, right or wrong, what you suggest is a definite possibility. It's a lot easier if you're dealing with new combinations of topics or a new approach than if you're adopting an unpopular point of view, since some teachers may feel that their own point of view is the only correct one. If that kind of instructor is, for example, strongly antifeminist, it's courting disaster to turn in a paper that attempts to prove that the best poets were all women—no matter how good a case you think you can make. We know at least one instance in which an A-quality paper lost substantial credit for taking an original point of view that the teacher felt was absurd. It was the student's own fault. He'd sensed all along that he was bucking the teacher's prejudices.

STEP 6

Chart Your Course

You've already spent fifteen minutes or more on your paper, and all you have is one idea. Now we're going to ask you to spend some more time working up an outline before you start writing. You're probably wondering how all this will help you find more ideas. Unless you're a natural-born talent (in which case you don't need us), hang in there. You've also probably never written two sweat-free grade-A papers in a row. The *key* to generating ideas is to make an outline, so grit your teeth and follow along.

Way back in third or fourth grade, the Mrs. Smiths of this world taught us all how to outline. They insisted that we outline every 100-word paper, predicting that outlining would be useful all through school.

But 100-word papers really didn't need to be outlined, except perhaps in our heads, so as we sailed through the rest of elementary school and maybe even junior high, we forgot outlining along with such similarly useful skills as how to make a city out of wooden blocks.

Your inability to start a paper without sweat and procrastination is Mrs. Smith's revenge.

If your paper is just a paragraph, you still don't need to write down an outline. If you're writing less than 300 words, you can probably outline just by jotting down a few facts that prove your main idea. (If you've got a good memory, you may be able to outline in your head.) But if your paper is to be more than 350 words, a formal preliminary outline is the quickest, easiest, and most effective way to organize all the thoughts that ought to be rattling around in your head—or to prod loose some thoughts from your unwilling brain.

If you're adept at outlining, you can choose any form that's comfortable for you. If you haven't done much outlining, start with the same formal letter-and-number outline your Mrs. Smith probably preferred:

Formal Outline Format

I. Subtopic
    A. Fact
        1. example
        2. example
    B. Fact
        1. example
        2. example
        3. example
    C. Fact
        1. example
        2. example
II. Subtopic
    A. Fact
        1. example
            a. subpoint
            b. subpoint
        2. example

(etc.)

Whichever way you outline, follow these four guidelines:

1. Write legibly, and on paper that's large enough and permanent enough that it won't get lost. You're going to need to refer to the outline as you write your paper, and to check against it before you hand in your work.
2. Leave plenty of blank space on the page so that you can shift around the order of your points or substitute one for another as you write.
3. Be sure to write down a few words to remind you of each subtopic that you intend to deal with in your paper. Remember, subtopics are always *ideas.* Also jot down, in a word or two, every fact that you'll use to demonstrate, explain, or prove that idea.

Since all ideas are a matter of opinion, they're going to have to be defended. You defend with the facts: examples, statistics, and so forth. Notice that the standard outline form shown above reminds you that you're going to need those facts. In addition, some ideas need to be explained in more concrete language, with examples of what you mean.

Keep in mind that if a *fact* is not generally accepted (at least, not by your grader), you're going to have to prove that, too, in your paper. You can prove it by citing the steps in your own research, or with a quick citation from an authoritative source (book, journal, or person of authority).

4. When you outline, keep in mind the length of your paper and don't take on too much. The chart on page 45 will help you gauge whether or not you're trying to tackle too many ideas. (These are not hard and fast numbers, just guidelines.)

As you can see from the chart, a good paragraph-length assignment contains only one idea and has no other space for unproven facts or opinions. So once you've got your idea

Average Expected Number of Ideas and Facts for Papers

Word length	*# of subtopics*	*# of details*	*# of examples*
50 to 150	none	3	0 to 1 for each fact
150 to 350	0 to 1	3	1 for each fact
350 to 750	2 or 3	3 for each	1 or 2 for each
800 to 1,250	2 or 3	3 for each	1 to 3 for each
1,250 or more	3 or more	3 for each	3 for each

you can just put it down in sentence form and get on with the facts that support it. If you prepare a scrap-paper outline, it might look like this:

All continents were once joined
1. same fossil plants all over the world
2. continents fit like puzzle
3. mid-ocean ridge pushing both ways

The outline for a short paper can contain facts that take longer to prove:

Why children get the flu
1. exposed to other kids at school
2. immunity not built up
3. don't dress as carefully as adults

But even for a short paper, it's best to select facts that are accepted or provable with a single authoritative citation. An authoritative citation for the fact that children don't have strong immunity to flu could be, for instance, "Dr. James Kelsey, in an article in the *New England Journal of Medicine.*"

If you're writing a paper of more than 750 words, you're expected to have several ideas in it. It's also probably assumed that you're going to do some research. If so, it's a good idea to prepare a preliminary outline before you do your research, and to review both the working title and the outline before you begin writing. One or both may need adjusting to accommodate an idea or fact that you didn't think of before researching. If you've collected material mostly on one specific aspect of your title, you may even want to retitle your paper. Do it *now*.

15TH PROBLEM: When you think about subtopics, you go blank
SOLUTION: Ask questions about the title or the way the paper is arranged

A paragraph or short paper rarely presents any problems once you've got a title. Just write that main idea in sentence form and put in the facts that support it. But a longer paper requires several *subtopics* and you must come up with separate but related ideas for each one. That's where many people freeze up.

You can get your subtopics simply by asking questions about the title, or by arranging the paper in a specific way. The way it is arranged and questions to be asked depend on the category of paper you're writing.

1. FINDING SUBTOPICS FOR DIRECTION-GIVING PAPERS

For the paper that gives *directions,* your subordinate ideas are the steps that lead the reader toward your goal—and they're written in the precise order in which they're to be done. To fill out your outline, just list those steps.

A simple step can be described in a sentence. A complicated step can take a paragraph to show. Don't worry at this stage if you can't fill in many facts or examples. Concentrate on outlining all the steps in their correct order. Where you're not sure of something, be sure to leave blanks, draw lines, or put in question marks—anything to remind you that those are points you'll have to research. Take along your outline when you *do* research, and you'll know just what information to look for.

If you can't easily jot down enough steps to fill the size paper you're writing, you can add length by breaking your topic into subtopics for which the steps are not all exactly alike. For instance, for a paper on "How to Patch Walls," the topic "Walls" can be broken up into plaster walls, concrete walls, and brick walls—or the topic "Patches" can be broken up into small patches, medium patches, and large patches.

If your assignment calls for a short direction-giving paper, choose a procedure that has just a few steps—or keep your instructions general.

Here's an outline we prepared for a straightforward direction-giving paper of 1,500 words on a topic we knew fairly well. For a shorter paper, we could have left out some of the kinds of patches we cover, or could even have lumped all the patches together. But we could not have left out any of the *steps* in telling how to patch, since the point of the paper is to give good instructions.

How to Patch Plaster Walls

I. Preparation for all plaster patching
- *A. Tools needed*
  - *1. Spatula or trowel*
  - *2. Sandpaper*
  - *3. ??*
- *B. Patching products to buy*
  - *1. Patching plaster*
  - *2. Glazol*
  - *3. Spackle*
  - *4. ??*

II. Patching cracks
- *A. Hairline cracks*
  - *1. Spread putty with fingers*

2. ??
3. ??
B. Deep cracks
1. ??
2. ??
3 ??
C. Wide cracks
1. ??
2. ??
3. ??
III. Patching holes
A. Small holes (similar to wide cracks)
B. Large holes
1. Cut plasterboard to studs
2. Cut new piece of plasterboard
3. Nail in new plasterboard
4. Feather edges
a. Layers of spackle
b. Feather each layer
c. Sand
d. Repaint

If your how-to is for an *intangible* course of action, there are no obvious sequential steps. To figure out what steps you need to show, ask yourself some questions, using the following clue words to help you:

where
when
what
why
how
who—if it applies to your title

Then arrange your answers (the subtopics) in some logical

order. If you need help with logical order, refer to the checklist on page 57.

Not all the preceding questions need be answered in any paper, but your paper must contain *some* of the answers. Notice how these clue words were used to prepare the following preliminary outline (later changed a good deal) for a 2,000-word article we wrote giving instructions on how to study more effectively (*Seventeen,* Sept. 1976). Notice also how we made the paper longer by breaking the topic "what to study" into its component parts: notes and books (subtopics V and VI).

How to Study More Effectively

I. Where to study
- *A. ??*

II. When to study
- *A. For lecture classes*
- *B. For recitation classes*

III. When not to study
- *A. ??*

IV. How to use study time
- *A. How long to study*
  - *1. what about all-night cramming?*
  - *2. ??*
- *B. How to keep studying*
  - *1. ??*
- *C. What about study breaks?*
  - *1. as reward*
  - *2. as necessity*

V. How to study notes
- *A. How to take notes*
  - *1. special paper?*
  - *2. pen or pencil?*
  - *3. note-taking shorthands*

B. *How to use notes*
1. *how to memorize*
a. *memorizing tricks*
(1) *mnemonic devices*
(2) *acronyms*
2. *??*
VI. *How to study books*
A. *Underlining*
1. *pros*
2. *cons*
B. *Writing in margins*

2. FINDING SUBTOPICS FOR REPORTS

Since a report is a description of events that have happened, the "ideas" in it are all factual. Since they happened in a time sequence, one event leading to the next, that's how they should be outlined. It's easy to prepare an outline simply by making every significant shift in time or place a different subtopic. Just ask yourself what happened first and where, and then what happened next and where—until you get to the last thing that happened. (If two things happened in different places at the same time, you may decide to describe all the events in one place, and then shift to the other place and do a flashback.)

Here's how we'd have outlined the body of a long report on automaker John De Lorean's drug bust (*Time* magazine, Nov. 1, 1982). Many of the "facts" in the outline are more detailed explanations of *what* occurred, but some answer the questions *why, how, where,* and *when.*

Notice that at least one explanatory detail (which we've starred) is not part of the actual series of events. Instead, it bolsters a secondary angle—that the FBI was caught off-guard. Notice also that no information was included in the outline about *why the event was significant.* That belongs in the *introduction* to the report. (We'll talk about introductions in another section.)

Working title: How John De Lorean Was Caught

I. Drug Enforcement Administration got leads to Hetrick
  A. who Hetrick was
  B. how DEA found him
II. DEA learned details of Hetrick's schemes
  A. dope importation scheme
  B. money laundering scheme
III. FBI called in, joint surveillance done
  A. dupe set up to "help" with money-laundering
    1. De Lorean, friend of dupe, wanted in
      *a. surprise of authorities at this turn of events**
    2. De Lorean–dupe meeting taped by FBI
    3. De Lorean, Hetrick met to talk terms
  B. money and drugs were exchanged
    1. where
    2. when
  C. step-by-step description leading to arrests

3. FINDING SUBTOPICS FOR EXPLANATIONS OF IDEAS

For every paper that deals with ideas (even a paragraph), it's especially important to give the three levels of information Mrs. Smith taught in her outline form: (1) a general statement of idea, (2) specific facts that show or prove it, and (3) examples or proofs for each specific fact. Though you need not refer in your outline to the examples you intend to use, it makes the actual paper-writing go faster if you do. If you stick to the rule of three-level writing, we guarantee that you'll never get back a paper with the comment "unconvincing" or "lightweight."

For papers that explain ideas (as well as intangible actions like how to study), you've got to impose some logical order on the material, such as moving from easy information to hard, or grouping similar thoughts close together. (The "How to Study" outline moves along roughly in the sequence in which the techniques need to be used.) The chart at the end of this section lists some of the logical sequences that are most frequently used. If you're stumped for a plan, prod your brain by going down the list. One helpful device is to make questions with the words:

- What's *good and bad* about the (title)?
- What *caused* the (title)?
- What's *known* about the (title)?

Another way to find subtopics is to ask the familiar questions *what, who, where, when, why,* and *how* about the title. You can even combine one of those words with one of the organizational formats we've listed. Here are some examples of how to do that:

- *What* are the *pros and cons* of (fill in your topic)?
- *When* did (your topic) become recognized?
- *Why* is (your topic) important?
- *Where* did (your topic) get *started*?
- *How* was (your topic) *caused*?
- *Who* is the most *controversial* (your topic)?

In addition, there's one question all papers about ideas should answer: *So what?*—in other words, why is it important to understand this idea? It's a question that most students forget to answer. It usually belongs in the paper's introduction. Be sure to include it in *your* paper; then watch the grader sit up and take notice.

Here's our preliminary outline for a 3,000-word article we prepared for *OMNI* magazine (Dec. 1981). Since we knew very little about the topic before we started researching, we made several kinds of notes to ourselves to get needed proofs and examples. Like the "How to Study" outline, it's more complicated than you'll be expected to prepare for anything but a term paper or thesis. Nonetheless, it shows several patterns of organization and is worth studying for that.

Agent X: Biology's Subatomic Particle

I. What is it?
- *A. Its chemical composition*
  - *1. proof from authority*
- *B. Where it's found*
  - *1. __________*
  - *2. __________*
  - *3. __________*
- *C. What diseases it causes (for sure) (get specifics)*

II. Who studied the particle
- *A. Labs where people are working on it*
- *B. Research techniques tried*
- *C. Typical experiments*
  - *1. Historical*
  - *2. Now*

III. Importance of understanding the particle
- *A. To science and medicine*
- *B. To mankind*
- *C. To people researching it*
  - *1. Nobel prizes, etc.*

As you develop your outline, you may find that one kind of organization works best for one part of your paper, and another kind for the rest. It's okay to change interior organizational patterns from one main topic to another. (In the De Lorean outline, the first subtopic contains *who* and *how,* and the third subtopic contains *sequential* events.) But make sure to stick to one and only one organizational pattern for all your main topics. (In the De Lorean outline, the main topics are sequential.) The more evident the patterns are to the reader, the easier your paper will be to follow—and the higher your grade will be, too.

4. FINDING SUBTOPICS FOR THE PERSUASIVE PAPER

Remember that the persuasive paper is actually one of the other four basic types of paper (usually explanatory) with an obvious point of view added to it. Your introduction and ending show your point of view, but the body of the paper is generally written just as if it *were* the other type of paper. There are only two extra added ingredients:

- You must include at least three pieces of evidence that support your point of view.
- You must deal with the opposition, presenting and refuting the other side of the issue.

Otherwise, the grader will take away points for failing to convince adequately.

Here's a preliminary outline for a persuasive paper of about 600 words:

Skiing Is Good for the Heart
I. Aerobic value
A. skiing is aerobic
1. (proof)
2. ___________
B. aerobic exercising benefits heart
1. (proof)
2. ___________
II. Cold weather's value
A. skiing is done in cold weather
B. cold weather's benefits to heart
1. (proof)

III. Cold weather: a strain on heart?
A. evidence that it is
B. evidence that it's not

5. FINDING SUBTOPICS FOR A SHORT STORY

A short story is a fictional series of events. To outline it, ask the same questions you'd ask if you were preparing a report.

★ ★ ★

To get some hands-on practice in finding subordinate ideas, stop for a few minutes now and select subtopics for your own title. Then prepare an outline for a medium-sized paper.

16TH PROBLEM: The topic is too specific for a long paper
SOLUTION: You probably need more facts and examples

We don't believe there's *any* topic that can't be discussed in at least a thousand unpadded words. We've taken one incident and broadened it into several 1,000-word articles. Then we've taken the 1,000-word articles and made them into 50,000-word books. In fact, most professional nonfiction writers find it much harder to condense a paper into 500 words than to write 2,000 words about the topic.

Why are you having problems? For one of two reasons. Either you haven't got enough *facts* and *examples* (which usually means you don't know enough about the topic and had better do some more research before you write) or you are mistaking an *example* for an *idea.*

To review: *An idea is something that hasn't been proven.* If you're not sure of that, review the titles that have been suggested throughout this book.

An example is a specific piece of information. Here are some *examples:*

1. HUD is an acronym for the Office of Housing and Urban Development (an example for use in the "How to Study" article).
2. To make large batches of Agent X for his first experiments, Dr. Stanley Prusiner began by injecting mice with brain material from sheep that had a disease called scrapie (an example for use in the "Agent X" article).
3. According to Dr. Kenneth Cooper, author of *The Aerobics Way,* exercise strengthens the heart if you breathe deeply while you're doing it (an example for use in the "Skiing" paper).
4. Spread patching compound both in the opening of the hole and around its edges (an example for use in the "Patching" paper).

If you keep this difference clearly in mind, you'll never again have papers returned labeled "padded."

17TH PROBLEM: Where to put ideas that aren't part of the main idea
SOLUTION: Make each idea into one or more subtopics or subpoints

We pointed out, way back, that the persuasive paper titled "Voters Don't Know How to Choose Good Representatives" hides a second idea that has to be dealt with: *how voters do choose their representatives.* To write most persuasive papers, you must explain what you're talking about before you can take a position on it. It stands to reason that your first one or more subtopics has to be used to explain your idea.

Notice that the persuasive paper "Skiing Is Good for the Heart" has a secondary idea that must be explained first: *what skiing does to the heart.* We divided what it does into two parts, an exercise component and a cold-weather component, and then we assigned each component to its own subtopic.

Ideas that aren't strictly part of the topic come up in all kinds of papers including direction-giving papers, reports, and explanations. The outline for "How to Study More Effectively" deals with an idea that's not strictly part of the main topic: *when not to study.* Notice how it's inserted in the outline.

In the De Lorean outline, there's a secondary angle that's not stated clearly as a subtopic but only implied by the use of a fact. It's point III.A.1.a.: *surprise of authorities at this turn of events.* Skilled professional writers—especially fiction writers—gain subtlety in their writing when, instead of stating subordinate ideas outright, they just put in the facts (often as scenes, dialogue, or description) that lead the readers to come, on their own, to the author's own controversial or surprising conclusions. It's a difficult trick, but you might enjoy experimenting with it.

Checklist for Organizing Papers or Sections of Papers

GROUP 1. In time sequence:

- in the sequence in which it was seen or done
- in the sequence in which it should be seen or done
- from cause to effect
- from start to finish

GROUP 2. From general to specific:

- general topic to subtopics
- theoretical to practical
- generalizations to examples

GROUP 3. From least to most:

- easiest to hardest
- smallest to largest

- worst to best
- weakest to strongest
- least complicated to most complicated
- least important to most important
- least effective to most effective
- least controversial to most controversial

GROUP 4. From most to least:

- most known to least known
- most factual to least factual (fact to opinion)

GROUP 5. Giving both sides (grouped or interspersed):

- pros and cons
- similarities and differences (compare and contrast)
- assets and liabilities
- hard and easy
- bad and good
- effective and ineffective
- weak and strong
- complicated and uncomplicated
- controversial and uncontroversial

STEP 7

Formulate Your First Words

If you can't write an introduction in five minutes, you're trying too hard. For most school papers, you'll get a high grade if you simply take a forthright approach:

1. State the topic and your approach.
2. Tell why you've chosen this particular topic (unless it was specifically assigned just the way you're writing about it).
3. Explain why you've chosen this particular angle (unless it, too, was specifically assigned).
4. Briefly summarize—in the most general way you can find—the ideas you've got in your outline.

Here's a complete introduction for a short paper on How to Patch Plaster Walls:

> Few people know how to patch plaster walls, but it's something most of us must do sooner or later. With the right tools and the right patching products, patching most holes is easy.

The first sentence answers points 1, 2, and 3 listed on page 59. The second sentence answers point 4. And, with the help of our outline and working title, the whole thing took three minutes to write.

For a short paper, keep your introduction short. For a long term paper or a thesis, your introduction can run several paragraphs in length because you may have to use several facts and some examples in defending your reason for choosing the topic. For instance, *Time* magazine spent half a dozen long paragraphs on a thorough biography of millionaire John De Lorean in order to explain why *his* drug bust was worth a cover story even though few drug busts are reported by *Time*.

Fiction generally has no introduction. The best technique is to begin where the action in the story starts, and then to fill in "introductory" material at the point where each bit of information becomes important in explaining what's going on.

18TH PROBLEM: The introduction has to be extra special
SOLUTION: Start with a lead

Lead is the word used in newspaper and magazine writing for the catchy introduction to an article—the grabber that makes people read past the summary we've described above, and keep going until the end of the paper. Some books list a dozen different kinds of leads, but they all fall into one of two basic categories:

- They appeal to the reader's intellectual curiosity
- They appeal to the reader's emotions

There are three easy ways to appeal to curiosity: (1) ask an interesting question, (2) make a surprising statement, or (3) pose a paradox (two statements that seem contradictory).

But if you ask a question, you must answer it later to the reader's satisfaction. If you make a surprising statement (a description of something unusual, a hint at controversy, or even just an unknown fact), you must back it up with proof somewhere in your paper. And if you put together a paradox, the supposed contradiction must be explained away later on.

Examples of this kind of introduction abound in popular magazines. Here's one for an article by Alan D. Haas* on the value (*angle*) of collecting antique cars (*topic*). Note the use of startling statistics, eye-catching questions, and even a surprising statement from an expert, all leading to the author's summation in the final paragraph. Note, too, the way the author's point of view shines through in his choice of words: *astonishing price, lovingly restoring, original beauty, splendid machines.* It's those attitudinal words that give his writing character and verve. Take them out—in other words, try to eliminate point of view—and what's left is bland writing.

> If you had purchased it in 1972 for $50,000 you could have sold it currently for $235,000. What is it?
>
> A Picasso or other modern painting? A Russian sable fur, a rare diamond or postage stamp, a mansion in Beverly Hills, several gold bricks?
>
> No; none of these. The answer: an eight-cylinder, 1932 Duesenberg Phaeton SJ-261 vintage automobile, sold at auction in the Midwest for this astonishing price—highest dollars ever paid for a classic American car.
>
> According to Frank (Skip) Marketti, director of the Auburn-Cord-Duesenberg Museum in Auburn, Indiana, where the auction took place, "Duesenbergs have increased at least 20 percent in value each year of the past

**Science Digest,* March 1979. Copyright 1979, Alan D. Haas. Used with the author's permission.

> ten years." This particular Duesenberg appreciated even more because its owner, Ed Lucas, an engineer in Detroit, spent thousands of hours lovingly restoring it to its original beauty.
>
> What was formerly a hobby, the collecting of Locomobiles, Cords, Bugattis, Isotta Fraschinis, for the pleasure of owning, tinkering with, or simply admiring these splendid machines of the past, has, in the past decade, become a bonanza for knowledgeable car freaks.

The second approach, appeal to the emotions, is actually a stronger grabber than appeal to the intellect, if it's used well. It's especially popular in the personal experience paper, but just as useful in any other kind—just so long as you don't try to be too dramatic. Heavyhanded drama turns graders off.

Dramatic overkill sometimes even gets into print. We once saw a lead in a medical journal that described a tense airplane scene, a near-mutiny by passengers at the end of a snowy Boston runway. The author kept his fingernail-biting drama unwinding for 200 words. But then he tried to tie the anecdote to his theme with a weak analogy: that American health care is like that tense airplane mutiny. What a letdown that was! Needless to say, we never read past the lead.

Your lead can appeal to any emotion: fear, pride, comfort, amusement, regret, vanity, and more. But if you choose a strong emotion, it's especially important not to seem to be manipulating readers' reactions. In addition, the appeal has to have something to do with the title. An appeal to fear in a paper warning of a life-and-death situation is probably appropriate. But an appeal to fear in a paper on American health care may make the reader expect satire.

One sure emotional appeal is flattery, and it works especially well with graders—so long as you use it subtly and appropriately. For instance, if your instructor is a music lover, and you're writing a paper called "The Use of the Word 'I' in James Joyce's Ulysses," you might look for references to how Joyce felt about music when you do your research. If there's any reference that you can tie to the theme of your paper without stretching, begin the paper with it.

Anecdotes—little true stories—are a favorite lead technique of popular nonfiction writers. If you have a good true story about the topic, begin with that—but make sure that it really makes a point about the topic.

Here's how author Jack Galub used two anecdotes to lead into an article called "Summer Water Safety—Amazing New Facts That Can Save Your Life."* They both make the point that drowned people *can* be revived. (The article goes on to describe this fact, and others, that "can save your life.")

> The child was found unconscious in a backyard pool. She had been underwater for possibly 15 minutes. Resuscitation efforts failed. But minutes after being given up for dead, the drowned two-year-old began to breathe. Sixteen hours later, she recognized her mother and spoke to her. A two-year follow-up showed the child growing normally, with no sign of brain damage.
>
> An 18-year-old drove off a country road and crashed to the bottom of a 10-foot-deep, iced-over pond. Lifted out of the water 38 minutes later, he gasped spontaneously despite no detectable life signs. Intensive resuscitation efforts by a team of doctors started his heart beating. After two weeks, he returned to college, continuing as an A student.
>
> These lives were saved by the "mammalian diving reflex"—an involuntary reaction developed by whales, seals, porpoises, sea lions, and other animals that remain under water for extended peiods of time. The reflex is present in all mammals, and recent discoveries confirm

---

**Family Circle,* June 26, 1979. Copyright 1979, Jack Galub. Used with the author's permission.

that it can operate in some human beings, especially those under age 20, when they are plunged facedown into cold water.

As you can see, leads usually take at least 50 words—and can run as much as 500. Therefore they don't work well for papers that total less than 400 words. But for a longer paper—especially a term paper or thesis—they're a good way to catch the interest of someone who's grading a hundred papers. Keep in mind, though, that just a catchy beginning is not enough for an introduction. You must also include points a, b, c, and d that we described at the beginning of this section. And your lead must show the importance of the topic or illustrate your angle.

To get some practice now, take five minutes to write a simple introduction for the working title you picked earlier in the book.

STEP 8

Build the Body

Building the body of a paper is just like building the body of a car. You can do it as painlessly as if you were a robot standing on an assembly line—and as quickly as your fingers can write or type—once you've got a careful, complete outline. It all boils down to filling in the blanks. That's because the step right after your introduction is to write down everything in your outline in complete sentences or groups of sentences.

If you're writing a paper of less than 350 words, you may have the outline in your head, not on paper. If it's in your head, are you crystal-clear about the points you expect to make and what order you're going to make them in? If you're not, we urge you to take a minute to jot the ideas on paper before you start.

As you write, don't worry about spelling, punctuation, or grammar. You can fix all that later. Don't stop to hunt for the right word or phrase either—instead, if you need a reminder, put a question mark in parentheses at each place that you think can be improved. Your main attention should be focused on writing down the *ideas* you have, along with the facts that bolster your ideas. You can polish your prose when you do your editing and rewriting.

Rewrite? We can hear you groaning—at least those of you who've rewritten one or two papers in your school careers. Yes, rewrite. Try it once our way and you'll find that, in the long run, you *save time.* If you know that you're going to *rewrite,* you can be as messy as you like just as long as you can read it later. However, if your first draft is what you're planning to hand in, you have to do all the creative thinking and word-choosing *in your head* before you make a mark on paper—and then take more time figuring out how to write around any dumb words or phrases that you put down.

We recommend, too, that you type the first draft. Some writers do well writing longhand, but we've found that students who learn to think of words at the typewriter learn to get their ideas down faster because they can see whole pages of words at a glance. It's also a good idea to type (or pen) your first draft double-spaced or even triple-spaced, so that you have room between the lines to make revisions and insertions.

Look back at the outline we prepared (page 47) for a 1,500-word paper on "How to Patch Plaster Walls," and then at the introduction (page 59) that we typed for a 350-word paper on the subject. Here's what the first draft of the 350-word paper's body looked like:

> To patch most holes, you will need patching compound, gypsum board, a putty knife, and a knife. For ptching compound, you have three choices, each one just as good as the other. You can use a ready-mixed joint compound, which comes pre-mixed and ready to use, or powdered joint compound which must be mixed with water. It stores well, but it sets more slowly than ptching

plaster. You can use patching plaster to patch large holes and cracks. You have to mix it with water too.

To patch holes, make a neat rectangle around the damaged area. On a piece of gypsum board, lightly outline the size and shape as the rectangle, but don't cut it yet. First mark another boundary around the one you made, two inches from the line at every point. Cut on this line through the gypsum board. In other words, this piece is four inches wider and longer than the rectangular hole you made.

With a sharp knife, score lines for the plug through the first layer of paper, but don't cut the bottom later. Peel off the two-inch margin, leaving the bottom piece of paper intact. This is what holds the patch in place.

Next, spread patching compound around the opening and the edges and press the patch firmly in place, holding it a few minutes to set. Then spread patching compound over the entire patch, smoothing it out beyond the crack's edges. Smooth the edges so that the patch is even with the wall's surface.

That's all there is to it except for the ending—and the revision, which we'll save for later.

STEP 9

Conclude Concisely

The trouble with most endings is that they try to say too much. Here, for starters, is what an ending *shouldn't* do:

- It shouldn't contain any new ideas
- It shouldn't offer any new examples
- It shouldn't reach any new conclusions

Remember that everything you have to say—all your conclusions about the topic and your facts that prove them—belong in the body of the paper. The ending merely wraps up the theme and ties it in a bow.

The ending must be strong, but it mustn't be long. A sentence or two is often enough. The most popular endings follow one of the following patterns:

1. *Restate the purpose.* For instance, in the paper on patching plaster holes, you can end with, "That's all

there is to patching holes." If your paper's purpose was to persuade that autos should use gasohol, you could end, "As the evidence shows, gasohol is an environmentally valuable alternative fuel for autos."

2. *Sum up.* Wrap up all the points you've made into one general statement. For instance, for the same gasohol paper, a summary ending might be, "As the evidence shows, gasohol is safe, efficient, and a better user of natural resources compared to other automobile fuels." Short fiction sometimes ends with a summation: "She now knew she'd been dreaming all along" is an ending that's been used so often it's a cliche.
3. *Echo the lead.* A favorite of magazine writers is to end by repeating an image or phrase that was used in the lead. For example, this is how Alan D. Haas might have ended his article on the value of collecting antique cars: "Have you got an old Dodge Dart in the barn? Cherish it. Who knows when it could become another Picasso."
4. *Urge readers to act.* Tell what they can do to learn more about your theme, or, if it applies, simply say, "Go out and build yourself one."

STEP 10

Check for Quality Control

Before any car or toaster is permitted to leave the factory, it's thoroughly checked. If it performs poorly or looks shabby, it's sent back to be fixed. The more a manufacturer hopes to get customers to pay for the product, the more careful the quality-control inspection has to be.

You depend on customer approval even more than manufacturers do. The customer, in your case, is the person marking your paper. If your paper doesn't seem to be of high enough quality he may not bother to send it back to be fixed—but for each defect he'll definitely deduct from the grade he thinks the paper's worth.

Why pay, with a lowered grade, for the teacher to do your quality-control check? Learn to do your own editing.

Before you edit, it's a good idea to recheck what you've written against the outline to make sure that you've put in all the facts and examples that you originally decided to put in.

Then, if you have time, put your paper away for up to a week before you look at it again. It's amazing how a few days' distance permits you to see mistakes, weak links, and holes.

Then, to edit, simply check your first draft against the points listed below that apply to your paper, and make your changes in the spaces between the lines and in the margins of the first draft. When you're done, neatly copy the revised paper and hand it in.

Checklist for Editing

I. Structure
   A. The title
      1. Does it still show your entire idea (topic and approach) or is it too narrow?
      2. Does it still show only your idea, or is it too broad?
      3. Does it sound original? What makes it original?
   B. The introduction
      1. Does the introduction (or lead) show the topic and approach of your paper? Does it give the reason *why* this topic and approach are important? If your paper is an explanation, does it tell why it's important to understand this idea?
      2. If you've used a special lead to entice the reader, does it appeal to intellect or emotions? Is it effective? Have you kept it from being overly dramatic? Does it relate specifically to the main idea of your paper?
   C. The body
      1. Does it follow your outline?
      2. Is this the best logical order for your ideas?
      3. Are all the points in your outline covered?
      4. Are there other points that you now think should be added?

5. Are newly added points in the best place in the paper's body?
6. What logical patterns do you use:
   a. time sequence?
   b. from general to specific?
   c. from least to most important?
   d. or do you use another pattern?
7. Do you stick to one organizational pattern? If not, have you got a good reason for changing patterns, and do you give the reader clear guideposts for pattern changes?

D. The ending
1. Are there any new facts, new ideas, or new opinions? If so, take them out. (If they sound impressive—and stick to your main point—put them where they belong in the paper's body.)
2. Does the ending sound like a satisfying restatement, summation, echo, or suggestion?

II. Content

A. Facts
1. Check every fact to make sure that it's either a fact that everyone knows (or your grader accepts as proven), or that it has examples or other proof.
2. If most of your paper is made up of facts that don't need support, ask yourself, "What have I said that's new or worth writing about?"

B. Ideas
1. Does every idea say exactly what you meant it to say?
2. Are any ideas standing alone, without facts that support them? Do you provide enough facts? Do the facts really support the ideas, or are you stretching in places?
3. Do any ideas lead to conclusions you haven't included? Should they be included?

4. Are any ideas based on other ideas that you haven't included? Are you leaving out any steps in your argument?
5. Do any of the facts really lead to a different conclusion? Maybe they're in the wrong place in your paper.
6. Have you chosen the best facts for each idea? If some arguments seem weak, see if you can find more conclusive facts.

C. The grader
1. Do you assume that the grader is for or against your point of view? If against, are you convincing and is your grader open-minded about the theme of your paper?
2. Do you assume that the grader knows the subject? If not, have you explained basic facts that you know but she may not know?
3. Is your opinion kept out of the paper? Is your point of view shown just by your ideas, facts, and choice of words?

III. Mechanics
A. The paragraph: Does each paragraph have just one idea in it? Each paragraph should express just one idea—although you can use several paragraphs, if you need them, to fully support an idea.
B. Transitions: Transitional words and transitional sentences should connect your ideas. If there are any abrupt breaks or jumps between paragraphs—in logic or language—fill in with transitions.
C. Sentences: Sentences should be varied in structure and length. Are they?
D. Words
1. Are there any words that don't say precisely what you mean? Look them up in a thesaurus—the tongue-tied writer's godsend.
2. Does the spelling of a word look funny? Check it

in a dictionary. (You can catch spelling errors easiest if you've typed your first draft, since your eye is usually your best spelling-error guide.)

3. Is your grammar correct? Check your verb tenses. You know your weaknesses by now, so ferret out your mistakes before the grader catches them.

E. Punctuation: Check for too many dashes, too few commas, apostrophes in the wrong place, and quotation marks around words that don't need them.

19TH PROBLEM: The paper's not the right size
SOLUTION: Add or subtract facts, examples, and subtopics

You may have covered all the specific editorial points in the previous checklist, with your paper still ending up too long or too short to satisfy the assignment. Remember the rule that up to 10 percent wordage over or under the assigned length is generally acceptable. If you're still short, the easiest way to make a paper a little longer is to add another fact or example. A few more specifics generally add conviction to a paper, too.

If the paper's way too short, add length by discussing more aspects of the topic. For instance, if the paper was narrowed down to "The Use of the Word 'I' in *Ulysses,*" you could add a discussion of the use of related words. If the paper was narrowed to "A Report on Persons Killed at Gettysburg" you could add persons wounded there. Remember to change your title, introduction, and ending if you do broaden your original topic.

Another way to add a lot of length at one swoop is to bring in a second approach to the topic. For instance, a "Report on Persons Killed at Gettysburg" could include a "Description of the Battlefield by One of the Survivors." Just remember to justify the inclusion of this subtopic in your paper, and to make smooth transitions into and out of the subtopic.

If the paper's too long, reverse the procedure. If it's a little too long, see if you can simply tighten up your language by rewriting complex sentences and crossing out unnecessary words. If that doesn't condense it enough, delete a fact or an example—but make sure that you don't leave any idea undefended when you do. If it's much too long, look for an aspect or approach to delete, or see if you can combine two topics the way we combined small holes and large holes for our short paper on patching holes in walls.

★ ★ ★

We warned at the start that we wouldn't show you how to write paragraphs or how to structure sentences. It's beyond the scope of this book to attempt to bring your mechanics up to par. Instead, we've focused on the main point in writing papers—filling the page with ideas.

Now that you know what ideas look like, you probably see them all around you. If you have any about this book, we'd love to hear from you.

APPENDIX

Edited First Draft of Paper

Here's our edited first draft of the plaster-patching paper, from which we typed the final draft.

To patch most holes, you will need patching compound,

a pencil, a ruler, sharp a

gypsum board, a putty knife, and a knife. For ptching

there are

compound, ~~you have,~~ three choices, each one just as

s The first is

good as the other. ~~You can use a~~ ready-mixed joint

the

compound, which comes pre-mixed and ready to use. ~~or~~

third choice, a

powdered joint compound ~~which must be mixed with~~

a

~~water. It~~ stores well, but ~~it~~ sets more slowly than ptching

Your best bet is the second choice,

plaster. ~~You can use~~ patching plaster. To patch large holes,

It and patching plaster both have to be

~~and cracks.~~ ~~You have to~~ mix ed ~~it~~ with water. ~~too.~~

most draw
To patch holes, ~~make~~ a neat rectangle around the
with your pencil and ruler
damaged area. On a piece of gypsum board, lightly
in pencil of
outline the size and shape ~~as~~ the rectangle. But don't cut
, with the help of your ruler, draw a large rectangle
it yet. First ~~mark another boundary~~ around the one you
out
made, two inches from the line at every point. Cut ~~on~~
larger rectangle from
this ~~line through~~ the gypsum board. ~~In other words,~~ This
will be four inches
piece ~~is~~ four inches wider and longer than the rectangu-
lar hole you made. This piece is called the "plug."

cut along the smaller rectangle on being careful to cut
With a sharp knife, ~~score lines for~~ the plug, through
and the plaster. y of paper
only the first layer of paper, ~~but~~ don't cut the bottom layer.
from your inner rectangle
Peel off the two-inch margin, leaving the bottom piece
's larger rectangle margin
of paper intact. This is what holds the patch in place.

using your trowel, hole's
Next, spread patching compound around the opening
its Put on the patch and its margins,
and ~~the~~ edges. ~~and~~ press ~~the patch~~ firmly in place, hold-
until it s a thin layer of
ing ~~it~~ a few minutes ~~to~~ set. Then spread patching com-
the compound
pound over the entire patch, smoothing ~~it~~ out beyond
hole's Thin out the compound along
the ~~crack's~~ edges. ~~Smooth~~ the edges so that ~~the patch is~~
they are
even with the wall's surface.